Unpack Now

Get Rid of the Baggage in Your Relationships

Sedrik Newbern

O N E 11

One11 Publishing
872 S Milwaukee Ave, Ste 195
Libertyville, IL 60048

www.one11publishing.com

Publisher: Sedrik Newbern
Editor: Joanne Merry
Cover Designer: Joshua Swodeck

Printed in the United States of America
First Edition: April 2017

Author's Note
This book is based on my life experiences for learning and teaching purposes only.

ISBN Paperback 978-0-9982892-0-5
ISBN Digital 978-0-9982892-1-2

One11 Publishing is an imprint of
Newbern Consulting Group, LLC.

Dedication

This book is dedicated to my amazing wife. You have taught me so much about relationships and how to love by the way you love me and our son. Your love and support means more to me than I can ever express. I love you to infinity!

Contents

Acknowledgements   i

Introduction   iii

Focus on what's ahead   1

How I found LOVE   3

The sun will come out tomorrow   6

Your past should guide you, not define you   12

To overcome you have to let go   15

How to defeat fear   20

No fees for extra baggage   23

Too much, too little, too late   26

Just follow the directions   30

I hear you   32

Do they pass the relationship test?   35

Men are too indifferent   38

Who's on your team?   40

About the author   43

Acknowledgements

I thank God every day for bringing my wife, Denise Newbern, into my life. Now I know He was preparing me to be the man I need to be for you in all the experiences I have faced in life. You continue to inspire and amaze me with the support you give me on this journey to help others find restoration from broken relationships. This ministry continues to grow and make a lasting impact because of your prayers, guidance and continued support.

Matthew, you have given my life meaning since the day you were born. Son, you are my greatest accomplishment in life and I'm so proud of the young man you are.

I want to thank my family and friends for all of your support and encouragement.

To my wife, Denise Newbern; business manager, Samuel Watkins; consultant, DeShana Johnson; editor, Joanne Merry; graphic designer, Joshua Swodeck; cover model, Chara Swodeck; thank you all for the prayer, time, creativity, patience, support, and honesty you provided in the creation and design of this book.

Introduction

Do you feel broken? Are you finding it difficult to trust others because of the pain you still feel from previous relationships? Does it feel impossible to move on?

So many of us are broken. We are surrounded by brokenness throughout our lives. We then pass the pain of our brokenness from relationship to relationship and even to our children. We accept brokenness as reality and don't trust anything or anybody that disproves this in our lives.

How would you like to be restored?

I believe restoration is possible for those ready to move on. In this book, I share personal stories and provide tips on letting go. These experiences have helped my wife and me remove many of the roadblocks we encounter in our relationship. We have accepted the fact that we both brought too much baggage into our marriage, so we have had to unpack years of pain, mistrust and unrealistic expectations that we've packed away over the years from previous relationships. We have also agreed to help each other unpack by being supportive, understanding, and patient as we deal with each other and our emotions.

It is my prayer that through my experiences you find the inspiration and tools you need in this book to let go, move on, unpack and remove some of the baggage in the relationships in your life.

Focus on what's ahead

Imagine yourself behind the wheel of your
car. Instead of looking through the windshield,
you focus on the rearview mirror as you drive
most of the way. People, not just car safety
experts, would say this is not a very safe or
effective way to operate a vehicle. Aside from the
obvious danger this presents the driver and other
passengers on the road, focusing on the rearview
mirror will cause you to run up on obstacles, miss
your next turn and ultimately get delayed by
roadblocks you meet on your journey.

If this is true behind the wheel, then why do
so many of us go through life focused on the
rearview mirrors of our lives? Instead of looking
out on the horizon and dreaming of what's next,
we keep looking back at our past. We miss
opportunities to avoid obstacles and challenges,
because we are blinded by what happened to us.
The rearview mirror of our lives should only be
used to remind us of how far we have come and to

make sure that we have moved beyond the things we have left behind.

There's a reason the rearview mirror is only a fraction of the windshield size. You should live your life in the same proportion. You can't spend 90% of your time looking out of your rearview mirror. The life ahead of you is much bigger than your past, but you have to first focus on what's ahead.

Questions for Reflection

1. What is in your rearview mirror that keeps distracting you from what is ahead?

2. Think about a time when your focus on your past didn't allow you to fully embrace or enjoy your present circumstances. What did you learn from that experience?

3. How will you keep focused on your windshield of life instead of your rearview mirror?

How I found LOVE

LOVE is definitely in the air. However, for some, **LOVE** seems like just a dream, a fantasy. I felt this way after my divorce. I thought it was impossible to be in **LOVE** and happy. That is, until a conversation that changed my life forever.

Let's just say that I was in a very bad place in life and felt very alone. I had sworn off marriage. I didn't believe that a happy, long-lasting marriage was possible because of my experience and what I had seen others go through. I had resolved to be a bachelor for life. My family and friends didn't understand what I was going through and a few even distanced themselves from me at a time when I needed them the most.

I, however had one very special friend. She listened to me and saw past my pain. She helped me find my confidence and happiness again. One day in the park as we were having a heart-to-heart conversation about life and relationships, she taught me that it was possible to believe in **LOVE**.

She had also gone through a painful divorce. However, in spite of what she had gone through, she told me that she still believed in **LOVE** and one day she would get married again.

How was this possible? Why did she still believe in **LOVE** after divorce? I had so many questions for her and she had one simple answer... "I'm a good person and I deserve happiness." It was in this moment, that I realized the real meaning of **LOVE** – **Letting go** of the past, **Owning** your happiness, being **Vulnerable** with appropriate boundaries, and the ability to **Evolve**.

I'm happy to say that I celebrated my 10 year wedding anniversary in 2015 with my special friend. Because she believed in **LOVE**, she brought **LOVE** out of me!

Questions for Reflection

1. Do you believe it is possible to be in love AND happy in a relationship? If so, how does that look for you?

2. What does it look like to own your happiness?

3. How do you allow yourself to be vulnerable WITH boundaries?

The sun will come out tomorrow

We had just landed in Jamaica and the weather was absolutely terrible. From the moment we stepped off the plane, the rain continued to intensify all the way to our resort. Who wants to have a washed out vacation? But this wasn't just any vacation. In two days, we were getting married on the beach, so the weather had to be perfect or the wedding we had envisioned would be ruined. Was our wedding and ultimately our marriage going to be cursed? Is it possible that planning to get married on a Friday 13th guaranteed that things would not go well?

You have to understand that this was not the first marriage for either of us. We were both apprehensive about walking down the aisle again because it didn't work out as we had planned previously. In fact, we were engaged for about eighteen months before we even planned the wedding. While we both had opted for the more traditional wedding in our previous marriages, we decided on a destination wedding because we both had dreamed of an Oceanside wedding.

The arrangements with the travel agent went very well, including the price of the trip and accommodations for friends and family that wanted to witness this glorious day. The only exception was that there were no Saturday wedding slots available. When it comes to destination weddings, the resorts operate like clockwork with everything planned to the final detail and second. Each wedding is allotted a time slot and apparently Saturday the 14th was very popular. When the travel agent said that Friday was wide open, I didn't think anything of the day and said, "Let's book it!" It wasn't until I got off the phone that I realized I had just scheduled my wedding for Friday the 13th. I said to my fiancé (and myself), "the only reason we care about this date is because of a movie series that launched in the 80's. So if this was the mid 70's, we wouldn't care about the date."

So now we are 48 hours from our ceremony and Jamaica is getting pummeled with torrential downpours. We asked every employee at the resort if this was normal and they all said in their beautiful Jamaican accents, "Oh yes, this is just a little drizzle. But no worries, Mon; the sun will come out tomorrow!"

This was not true, because the next day we had yet another day of rain. As our friends and family began to arrive, they too got concerned about the possibility of a rained out ceremony. As we went to finalize the arrangements for the ceremony, we asked the wedding planner if she knew the forecast for our wedding day. She said, "Of course, it's going to be a beautiful day, Mon. No worries, the sun will come out tomorrow."

Now we are beginning to believe this is a scripted response that all employees are required to say to guests. Not to be fooled, we opted for our ceremony to take place at the gazebo instead of on the beach, so that we could take shelter in the event the rain was unbearable. We needed to be prepared just in case.

That night was so much fun! We hung out until the wee hours of the morning having the time of our lives. Again, we had been married before so all of the tradition of not seeing each other the night before and the day of were all tossed out the window.

The next morning I woke up around 5:30 am and I couldn't go back to sleep. I was so consumed with fear. Fear that the day would not go well because of the weather. Fear that getting married would somehow ruin the amazing relationship we had. Fear that my fiancé would wake up and decide that I wasn't the man for her.

It was in that moment that I got out of the bed and stepped onto the balcony overlooking the ocean. The first thing I noticed was that the rain had stopped. There was not a cloud in the sky. As a smile came over my face at the prospect of not having the ceremony washed out, I noticed that the sun was beginning to rise. I sat there and watched the most beautiful sunrise I had ever seen. As I sat in that moment, I began to pray and thank God for bringing me to this place in my life. I looked back in the room and saw this amazing woman that I loved with everything I had in me, sleeping like a princess with a little smile on her face. As I sat there reflecting, I felt tears rolling down my face knowing that I was truly blessed.

The day was absolutely amazing! We hung out at the pool before rushing off to the ceremony. The gazebo was the perfect backdrop for our ceremony and we took lots of photos on the beach. The best part was having dinner and then taking more photos as the sun set in the background. We couldn't have asked for a more perfect day.

In 2015, we celebrated our 10th wedding anniversary. Our lives have changed so much since that amazing week in Jamaica, but what hasn't changed is our love for each other and the genuine friendship that we share.

We often laugh about all the Jamaicans telling us, "Don't worry, Mon; the sun will come out tomorrow." Little did they know, they were speaking truth, not just about the weather but also about our lives and our future. It was dark and stormy for both of us before our relationship began. However, because of love, patience and communication we have been able to weather many storms. As a result, we are able to watch the sunrise in every aspect of our relationship.

I want to encourage you that if you are in the midst of a stormy season, "No worries, Mon; the sun will come out tomorrow."

Questions for Reflection

1. We all face storms and the unpredictability of tomorrow. How have you allowed storms to reshape your life in good and bad ways?

2. Knowing the outcome of these storms, would you change the way you approached them in hindsight?

3. Are you dealing with something today that you are not able to let go of? Where will you end up if you never let it go?

Your past should guide you, not define you

Do you remember the scar you got from the first really nasty fall you had on your bicycle? The pain and aches lasted for days. Then after the aches went away, there was that ugly scab that appeared covering up the wound. Your mom told you that the wound was healing but you could still feel pain when you touched the scab.

Then one day, you're outside playing and you had forgotten about the scab because it no longer hurt. That's when the scab got ripped off and all the pain came right back to you.

After this life altering experience, you decided to protect the wound no matter the cost. You wore Band-Aids, long pants and vowed to never to ride a bike again just as an extra precaution. Then finally the wound healed, the scab came off and you were left with a scar to remind you of the fall.

There's really no difference in healing from a fall off your bike and a fall in relationship. When a relationship is over, it hurts. Your heart aches for days, weeks, months and in some cases years. Then there's an ugly scab when you try to patch things up by going back only to be hurt again. Or your scab is the fact you refuse to tell your friends and family the truth about the relationship because of what they will say or think.

Then one day, you're finally outside playing again, trying to meet new people and even date. You've forgotten about the scab because you're enjoying the attention and the experiences. Then, something happens. You see a text, they say one thing and do something different, or you get a call from a friend telling you the person you're dating has someone else. The scab just got ripped off again. The pain comes rushing right back. You blame yourself saying that you should have known better and should have seen it coming.

Now you are protecting the wound no matter the cost. You have bandaged your heart and built a brick wall around it so that nobody can hurt you again. You have even vowed to never give anyone else 100% of you, because they will only hurt you again. Years go by and you find yourself lonely and still bitter. The wound has healed, but the pain left a scar in your life that reminds you of the fall you took in the relationship.

Broken relationships lead to life defining **PAIN**. The impact it has on your life can be negative or positive depending on how you deal with the **PAIN**. I challenge you to not let your PAIN define you!

PAIN can either make you **Powerless After Investing** in a **Negative** relationship or **PAIN** can give you **Purpose** and **Affirmation** to **Invest** in your **Next** choice. The choice is yours!

Questions for Reflection

1. How have you allowed PAIN to define your life?

2. In what ways do you find yourself taking your PAIN out on others?

3. What will change in your life when your PAIN gives you Purpose and Affirmation to Invest in your Next choice?

To overcome you have to let go

On a recent trip to Atlanta with my family, we decided to spend a day at the Andretti Experience playing video games and riding go-karts. It was the perfect day for a seven year old kid and his dad. Then just as we were about to jump in the go-karts, my son got scared and started yelling, "I can't do it! I can't do it, Dad!" I'm not sure where the fear came from and frankly we had to get past this because the dad really wanted to drive the go-karts! I encouraged my son by saying that he would be fine and there was nothing to worry about. I told him these go-karts were just a slightly bigger version of his small razor go-kart at home that he handles with ease. He finally got up the courage and jumped behind the wheel. In the end, he was my biggest competition on the course.

The story doesn't end there. The next adventure was conquering the zip line that was suspended over the tracks across the entire length of the building. This time it was not my son that needed encouraging… it was Dad who is not too fond of heights. As we waited our turn to get suited up, I watched the others going before me trying to calculate the height, speed and velocity. As we climbed the stairs to the launch point, I could feel my heartbeat increasing in intensity. I couldn't flake out on this after giving my son the best pep talk on overcoming your fears.

As I watched my son get hooked to the line and leap off the platform with the biggest smile on his face I saw in him pure freedom and excitement. Then my wife took off down the line screaming and laughing at the same time filling my heart with joy that I was experiencing such a fun day with them. Next up was our aunt (who is more like a big sister to my wife). Again, I saw on her face pure joy, but my heart was pounding so hard that I knew the kid behind me could hear it.

Then it was my turn. I stepped up to get hooked to the line and the guide mumbled something. Then, I felt a nudge in my back, but I braced myself so that I wouldn't launch until I knew for sure what his final instruction was for me. Upon repeating himself, he gave me a more forceful push and over the ledge I went. Now I'm gliding through the air 30 feet above speeding go-karts with just the support of a tightly secured harness attached to a wire.

That's when it hit me. I could succumb to my fears and panic with absolutely no way to get off the ride until it was over. Or I could embrace the moment and feel the same excitement and joy that my son, wife and aunt enjoyed. It was then that I yelled and began to laugh as I began to spin around while gliding down the wire. At first I thought I would feel safer if I could at least see the endpoint, but now I was facing back toward the launch pad. Now I could see the entire room and enjoy the cool breeze from the wind thanks to the velocity of my aerodynamic body quickly gliding across the facility.

Then in a flash, I came to a stop. The zip line was over and I actually wanted to keep going. When I came down the steps I couldn't help but notice the big grin on my son's face. He ran up to me, gave me a big hug and said, "Dad I knew you could do it!" That was a proud moment for me.

Here's what I learned from this adventure:

- Fear can keep you from having some of the best experiences of your life.
- It's great to have mentors and a support system that will encourage you and show you by example what you can accomplish when you overcome your fears.
- As you climb to new levels in life, you have greater fears to face like falling and failing.
- Often we need a nudge to get us over the edge to ultimately face our fears.
- Once we let go and embrace the experience, we begin to see things from a perspective we would have never seen.
- Every mentor needs coaching and encouragement too.
- I have the best son in the world!

This experience has not completely eliminated my fear of heights, but it has given me the courage I need to climb another flight of steps and to leap off the ledge knowing that in the end, I have the support and encouragement to keep me from falling or failing.

Questions for Reflection

1. What are your fears and what are they preventing you from enjoying?

2. Have you ever come face to face with your fear only to be pushed into facing it head on? How did this make you feel? What was the outcome of facing your fear in such a way?

3. Who do you have watching how you face your fears? What example are you setting for them and how can you help them overcome their own fears?

How to defeat fear

This idea will never work. I will never be successful. I always fail or come up short. My dreams never come true. Something always happens to throw me off my game.

Have you ever had these conversations with yourself? Do you find yourself filled with doubt as you enter challenging situations? When things don't go as well as you planned, do you remind yourself that you knew it wouldn't work?

We are often our own biggest critics. Even when we have a corner filled with supporters and encouragement, we still listen to the voice in our head that tells us we can't. The voice points out all the times we didn't succeed. The voice only focuses on the people around us that say we will fail. The voice finds all the statistics that prove success is impossible. The voice just gets louder and louder until it drowns out logic and excitement and our desire to succeed. The voice is best known as fear.

Tips to Defeat Fear

Focus on Your Destiny

I have found that when that voice gets loud for me, I begin to pray for wisdom and a renewed focus on my destiny. I know that my purpose in life and its impact on others is far greater than the fear that is trying to slow me down. I call this my reality check or slap in the face. When you are working for something greater than yourself that will impact others, your faith gives you the ability to harness the motivation to push through roadblocks like fear.

Measure Your Successes

I then shift my focus to aspects of my life that are within my control. I measure my successes and yes, I look at the glass as half full. Far too often, we feel defeated because we come up short of our expectations or things don't go exactly as planned. Instead of dwelling on the negative, look at what you did accomplish. For some, just trying something new and different is an accomplishment. You also have the benefit of the experience and knowledge you gained so that next time you will have better success and avoid the potential pitfalls.

Seek Support

Whenever I face challenges, I seek out those that have traveled similar paths for mentoring and coaching. I'm a firm believer in mentoring and coaching. Most successful people are more than willing to help others achieve success and this applies to business and relationships. There's also an abundance of resources available to guide you including books, articles and business/life coaches.

I encourage you to fight past the fear. Invest in yourself so that you can live into your destiny and have the impact on others you were created to make.

No fees for extra baggage

I think the airline industry has truly
capitalized on our inability to pack light and only
take the essentials on our journey. I will be the
first to admit that I am guilty of packing too much
because you never know what you might need
while you're away. As hard as I try to fit
everything into just one bag, I soon realize my
luggage is overweight and difficult to close. I have
no choice but to move some of my clothes into
another bag, and yes, fill this additional bag with
a few extra items that initially didn't make the
cut. Depending on the airline I'm traveling, this
could cost me an additional $25 - $35 per bag.

This entire experience reminds me of how
so many of us deal with the impact of our past
relationships. Over the years, we collect both good
and bad memories from each of our relationships
and we pack them into our hearts. At some point,
the memories become overwhelming for us and we
can no longer close them up in our hearts

securely. Instead of unpacking, we pick up another piece of luggage to hold all of our stuff. This happens over the course of many years and the bags begin adding up. Now the bags in our life are overwhelming and difficult for us to carry. Even though we have sincere offers to help us with our bags, we decline these offers, determined to manage our baggage by ourselves.

Now imagine if your boyfriends or girlfriends decided to no longer offer to help you unpack and carry your bags. What if they want more for you than you want for yourself? What if their actions only remind you of negative experiences you've been carrying around with you for 15 years? What if boyfriends charged you for extra baggage like the airlines? Could you afford the extra fees?

I believe that we have all of the essentials we need for our **Journey 2 Forgiveness** inside... we were born with them. Our problem is that we pack so many other issues in our hearts that the essentials are covered up and not available for use when we need them as adults.

It's time that you finally **Let It Go** and **Move On** once and for all!

Questions for Reflection

1. Do you believe it is possible to be in love AND happy in a relationship? If so, how does that look for you?

2. What is it that you can't let go of from the past? What is keeping you from making room for something new?

3. What positive and healthy experiences from past relationships can you list? How can you integrate these into expectations for a new and healthy relationship without alienating a potential mate?

Action step: Make your list. Pray for affirmation to keep the positive aspects from past relationships in your heart and remove the negative. Move forward with an open mindset.

Too much, too little, too late

Have you ever felt trapped in a dead end relationship? Has the romance faded so much over time that you don't see how to get it back? Are there just too many burned bridges for you to go back to the happiness you once shared? Can you identify with every lyric of the 1978 hit song "Too Much, Too Little, Too Late" by Johnny Mathis and Deniece Williams? I've been there. Many of my clients and friends have as well. The question is how do we get there over time and better yet, how do we recognize the path we are on to avoid the final destination?

Let's start with **Too Much**. Unfortunately, many of us spend too much time getting relationship advice from bitter people. You know who I'm talking about. This is the person in your life that has consistently failed at relationships or has remained in a toxic relationship for years. They love telling you what you need to do to avoid getting hurt and taken advantage of, but you have never seen them take their own advice. These people are in your family, in your church, on your job, at your kids sporting events and now, thanks to on-demand cable television and the internet, they are available 24/7.

Connect with other loving, spiritually-centered couples. Look for older, long-term couples to serve as mentors for you and your spouse. Keep in mind, every couple has problems. The key is finding couples that have found positive and productive ways to solve their problems together.

Too Little is always controversial. Relationships suffer when we give too little of our time and attention to ourselves and our relationships. The best moms typically get so lost in their children and all of their activities that they are too exhausted for a bubble bath or quiet time with their spouse and date nights just don't exist. Men tend to get so consumed in work trying to provide for the family, that we give too little attention to our wives. When men do have free time, it is spent on the golf course or pursuing a hobby that doesn't include our spouse.

Focus on quality time spent. Schedule weekly date nights with your spouse and preferably not just going to the movies. You need to find opportunities to look in each other's eyes and talk about things other than your children, bills and your crazy families. Use the time to share your dreams about your future as you once did when you were dating. In fact, you should treat every date night as if you have only been dating for a month. This could increase the compliments, flirting and affection which we all enjoyed early in the relationship and tend to miss the most over the years as they fade away.

Lastly, it's never **Too Late** to try again. Sure there may be challenges in communication or emotional scars from arguments that went too far with words that were spoken. However, I believe that you can heal, forgive and rediscover the person that you once fell in love with and ultimately dedicated your life to until death do you part.

Never give up, because it's not too late to try again. Stop allowing bitter people to define your relationship and how you handle the challenges that come your way. If you focus your time and energy on yourself so that you can find your happy again, people around you will feel better about themselves and treat you better as a result of your energy. Exhaust every measure to find happiness again, including relationship coaches and counselors, to make sure that you find the spark and encouragement you need to keep fighting for your relationship.

Questions for Reflection

1. How have toxic people impacted your relationships?

2. What does quality time look like for you and does your significant other know this?

Action steps: Remove toxic people from your life. Find positive relationship mentors. Schedule at least three hours of quality time per week.

Just follow the directions

Do you study the directions thoroughly before starting a project or leaving on a journey? Or do you simply dump all the parts on the floor and look at the pictures with the expectation that you can figure it out? Or better yet, do you just simply pull off with no idea how to get where you're going but excited about the adventure assuming that you will find your way?

When it comes to life, parenting and relationships, things are not as simple as putting together furniture from IKEA®. Even though the pictures of happiness and love shown by others seem easy to create, you will find that without directions there will inevitably be missing parts and things will not work properly even if it looks like the picture. Not to mention, that if you set out on a journey without a defined course of where you want to end up, you will find yourself lost because of the many wrong turns you'll make if you don't have a clear roadmap for your future.

So many of us ignore the directions and only refer to them once we find that things are not working or when we finally realize that we are lost. Instead of pulling your hair out and threatening to destroy or throw things away, try reading the directions first to make sure you know where you're going, what you need to do to make things work properly and avoid the need to start all over again.

Action Step: My challenge to you is to read the directions first. Do your research on being a great spouse and parent just as you read books and take courses to excel in your career. Invest in yourself by hiring a coach (I know one that is awesome, by the way), finding a counselor or therapist, joining a Bible study group and attending marriage and parenting retreats. This will give you the direction you need to be successful both personally and professionally, just as they have for me.

I hear you

Men just don't listen when women just want to be heard. Men generally want to fix the problem when women just want them to listen. Men hurt women with their words and women never forget.

So much is said about the challenges men and women have communicating with each other. There are countless books and articles written on the subject. We all want to know how to more effectively communicate our feelings with our significant others, so we absorb everything we can on the subject.

As any good student would do, we take all of this new knowledge and phraseology with us into the next difficult conversation we have with the person we love only to leave hurt, frustrated and disappointed that it didn't go as smoothly as the book described it would. Then we can't sleep that night analyzing the entire conversation trying to figure out what went wrong. Why didn't they respond the way they should have based on the communications strategies we implemented? That's when we realize that we need to do more research to determine how to better get our point across the next time there's a disagreement. When the next time comes around, we still leave feeling hurt, frustrated and disappointed and this happens over and over again no matter how many books and articles on communication we read.

Here's the problem. I don't think men and women have an issue communicating. We have an issue listening.

Men and women have a tendency to listen with ears from their past. What does this mean? If you hurt me with your words, I believe everything you say is going to hurt. If I share my innermost feelings with you and you treat me as if my feelings don't matter, then I'm going to forever be guarded when it comes to sharing my feelings with you. If you only focus on solving the problem but never say I'm sorry, it will always be difficult for me to believe that you are truly sorry for how you made me feel.

The fact is, you could have developed your listening ears from previous relationships and your new love doesn't stand a chance getting you to change your opinion. Now tell me, is that fair? Do you think that will lead to a productive relationship?

Next time you are in a difficult conversation with the person you love, pay attention to the ears you are using. Listen with your heart. Listen with compassion. Listen with forgiveness in mind. Remember that communication in relationships is more about what is felt and not being said.

Questions for Reflection

1. How do you react/respond when you feel you are not being heard?

2. Think about yourself and how you listen. Do you have negative experience that act as filters for what you hear from others?

Do they pass the relationship test?

In the honeymoon phase of relationships, things are perfect. People are typically on their best behavior. They say and do all the right things. They are attentive, passionate and sensitive to your needs. Then, they change. The newness and excitement wears off. You finally find out who they really are. This person has tricked you and stolen your heart. You are all in at this point so you want to make it work, but deep inside you know that it won't. How did you not see this coming?

As a relationship coach, I'm often asked for my opinion specifically on a guy's motives, thoughts, words and actions. In addition to the obvious differences in how we approach communication and express our feelings, there are common challenges that surface in the first 90 days of a relationship. If you pay attention to the signs, you will quickly see whether or not this is the guy that you will want to sit on the porch with, drinking lemonade and holding hands with when you're 80 years old.

I was in a deep discussion during a podcast about relationships with my good friend, Dana Simone, author of "What's in Your 24?" It was the week before Valentine's Day, and I was telling her about recent conversations with women expressing their frustration and depression with their current relationships or relationship status. The holiday was approaching and the loving couple ads were flooding all media outlets intensifying the relationship struggles these women were fighting.

Dana began to tell me that she has a **90 Day Exploratory Phase** when it comes to relationships. During this time, she does her due diligence to make sure that the man she is dating is legit relationship material before she gets too involved or overly connected and committed. I thought I would share her process for pre-screening men in the first 90 days of the relationship so that it will spark a conversation and help others that consistently get involved with the wrong people.

Dana's 90 Day Exploratory Phase

- Pay attention to his conversation focus to uncover hidden financial issues
- Assess the relationship with his mother
- Look him up in the sex predator/domestic violence database
- Evaluate his job stability
- Assess the intensity of any baby momma drama
- Find out about all of his offspring
- Run a background check

As you can see, Dana is thorough. Also, many of these can be used by men.

Question for Reflection

Do you believe that more people should implement a more rigorous process to get a better understanding of who they are getting involved with before they share themselves, their time, their bodies, their families and a portion, if not all of their futures?

Men are too indifferent

Women often say men are too indifferent. They want the men in their lives to talk more and share what's on their minds. Some men, however, just don't speak up and share what's on their mind when it comes to relationships, parenting or even plans for dinner. Men tend to choose their battles so they are not constantly disagreeing or arguing with the women in their lives. This communication preference, or lack thereof, can be very frustrating for women.

But what happens when men do speak up and voice their opinion and expectations for their relationships, intimacy, finances and communication? Some women don't know how to handle this. Instead of embracing this open communication, women sometimes tell men they are being too controlling and too demanding. Is this true or is this just your reaction because you were not expecting a response?

Now this is not to say that some men don't take their expectations in relationships beyond reality. I'm referring to those guys that are comfortable enough and committed to you such that they want to make sure that your needs and theirs are met. This is the man that is willing to slide out on a skinny branch to say what he really wants from the woman he is fully committed and dedicated to.

When a man is bold in stating his desires and expectations, the gesture is often received with apprehension and disbelief. At times, women get very concerned and guarded. Here's the problem. If he is willing to open this door, please be aware of his vulnerability and be open to what you hear. This door doesn't open often, and if he is met with resistance, he will not open it again in the near future. How you handle this moment will determine the level of communication you have with him moving forward.

Remember that in relationships, you get what you ask for AND are willing to receive.

Who's on your team?

Throughout our lives, we go through traumatic events that test us mentally and spiritually. It could be a painful divorce that breaks up not just the couple, but their families and friends. It could be the loss of a parent, spouse, child or any loved one to cancer or car accident. Or it could be the shock of being laid off from the job that you have given the best 20 years of your life. No matter the event, it hurts!

When you're in the middle of the storm, it's very lonely. I've been there... I know! You just want someone to lean on. You need someone to tell you that you will get through this. They don't have to have all the answers. They just need to show compassion, show you that they care about you and want what's best for you.

Unfortunately, some of the very people that you expect to be there for you will disappear when you need them most. Best friends and family members will literally disappear and even disown you when you are facing life's most difficult challenges. Again, I've been there... I know!

These experiences have truly shaped my life and my relationships. Moments like these were tough on my spirit, but I survived because I was able to forgive others. Trust me when I say it's not as easy as it sounds! But in the end, I had to focus on my pain and let it go. I knew that my circumstances were giving me the foundation and strength I needed to move forward. I also had to accept there are three types of relationships in my life and that I need to approach them accordingly.

What are the three types of relationships?

Cheerleaders – We all need cheerleaders around us. They have a knack for lifting our spirits and motivating us by cheering us on. However, the cheerleaders only stand on the sidelines and scream out their support. They won't get in the game to help you win.

Coaches – These are the people in your life that give you all the advice in the world whether or not they have had personal experiences to guide their "wisdom". Some coaches are supportive and encouraging like Phil Jackson, while others get in your face like Bobby Knight. No matter the style, they have the ultimate goal of getting the most out of you and giving you a successful game plan.

Teammates – Your teammates are in the trenches with you. They know their role and they play full out right beside you. They fight to the end and gladly shed their blood, sweat and tears to help you. Whether you win or lose, they are still right by your side supporting you and encouraging you to keep fighting.

Life happens, so we have to be prepared to deal with the challenges that come our way. Relationships can be one of our biggest challenges during our most vulnerable times in life. I encourage you to surround yourself with strong teammates to give you support, find the right coaches to get the best out of you and figure out a better way to identify the cheerleaders so that you can use them appropriately.

About the author

Sedrik R. Newbern is a successful business owner, author and John Maxwell Certified Coach, Trainer and Speaker specializing in recreating relationships. When Sedrik shows up, relationships are recreated into workable, productive alliances that produce measurable results for individuals and business people. Years of experience have taught Sedrik that personal and business difficulties always stem from relationships that are stuck, burdened and unworkable. This knowledge is what drives him to be the force that recreates relationships into something that is peaceful, productive, empowering and prosperous.

A recognized leader in business and personal relationship coaching, Sedrik has developed and conducted hundreds of workshops and inspirational keynotes. His keynote presentations, workshops and consultations are interactive, thought provoking and life altering. His style is authentic and engaging and he is driven by his mission to assist people in recreating the relationships in their lives and businesses into partnerships that work.

Relationship is fundamental to every aspect of existence as a human being. When relationships are draining, resentful, unforgiving and toxic, they become damaging to both individuals and businesses. Sedrik has an innate ability for identifying what isn't working and revealing it so that relationship can be recreated into something that is life-giving and empowering.

He serves on several non-profit boards and committees including serving as co-founder of The Precious Gift of Hope Foundation and as President for the University of IL Lake County

Extension Foundation. He also serves on the Tennessee State University College of Business Alumni Advisory Board and the Western Kentucky University Marketing Advisory Council. For his leadership in business and in the community, Sedrik has been recognized as one of Lake County Illinois' Most Influential African Americans, received the Alumni Achievement Award from Western Kentucky University Gordon Ford School of Business and received the Entrepreneur of the Year Award and Civic Leadership Award from the Chamber of Commerce.

A native of Nashville, TN, Sedrik holds a BS in Marketing from Western Kentucky University and an MBA with a concentration in Economics from Tennessee State University. He is the President and founder of Newbern Consulting Group, LLC as well as President of Phoenix Insurance & Financial Services, Inc. an Allstate Insurance agency in Libertyville, IL. Sedrik's success as an entrepreneur, he attributes to the support and motivation he receives from his wife Denise and their son Matthew.

For more information on his books, or to
invite Sedrik to conduct workshops and
motivational keynotes, please visit his website
www.sedriknewbern.com.

Other Books/eBooks by Sedrik Newbern

Unconditional Forgiveness
Lessons on Letting Go To Build Better
Relationships

How Did I Let This Happen?
5 Steps To Help You Move On

**Tips for Managing Social Media for Small
Businesses**
Co-authored with Scott Ventura, Integraphix

10 Free Marketing Tips
Co-authored with Scott Ventura, Integraphix

Stay connected with Sedrik

Twitter & Instagram – @sedriknewbern
Facebook – UnconditionalForgiveness
Facebook – SedrikRNewbern
LinkedIn – SedrikNewbern